Water Damage
& Other Poems
Consuelo

RIOT OF ROSES
PUBLISHING HOUSE
SEJATNGA
UNCEDED TONGVA TERRITORY
SOUTH WHITTIER, CALIFORNIA

Published by Riot of Roses Publishing House
Water Damage & Other Poems
Copyright © 2025, Consuelo de Veranó
ISBN (paperback): 978-1-961717-33-6
ISBN (ebook): 978-1-961717-34-3
Library of Congress Control Number: xxxxx

First Edition, 2025

To request permissions, you may contact the Publisher at riotofrosesllc@gmail.com
For bookings or interviews, contact: consuelodeverano@gmail.com

Printed in the United States of America
Edited by Annalicia Aguilar, Ghislaine LeFranc, and Brenda Vaca
Cover Illustration by Misty Crawford
Cover Graphic Design by Consuelo de Veranó
Layout Design by Consuelo de Veranó
Author Photo: Josue Emmanuel Muñoz
Other Photographs: Consuelo de Veranó

"*Water Damage* is a whirlwind look at identity. It feels like dipping your toes into a cold, calm ocean, only to look up and be hit by a wave of rushing, relentless water. Consuelo isn't only an artist and poet, but an introspective daydreamer whose words remind us that identity is as much human as it is magic. Every poem makes you feel like a tide that is taking you deeper into the ocean, only to release you back to land to reflect on what just happened. 'Sangre y Vida,' a short but powerful poem, serves as a reminder that we're all just water."

-Henry Leonor, Professor of English at Chaffey College

"*Water Damage* is a poetic prayer, drenched in honesty and divine insight, guiding us through both descent and ascension with 'feet pointed at heaven.' [Consuelo] shares revelations from encounters with guardian angels and demons, blurring the lines between the two. She reflects the ambiguous nature of relationships, and scrutinizes religious myths, only to 'burn them all down' and rise out of the debris with a vigorous faith in the future."

- Adam D. Martinez, author of *Remyth: A Postmodernist Ritual*

To my ancestors and elders—
wouldn't be here without them.

To queer and trans people everywhere—
we are, and that will not change.

To poets, deviants, and ethical sinners—
luv you <333.

The Damage Catalogue

Prologue

3.   Water Damage

Hospital de Mentiritas

9.   In the Beginning... (Genesis 1:1)

10.   An Epitaph

11.   She Had Love For All

14.   Fucking Vegans (Are Trying To Kill Me)

16.   Ostrich

18.   Depression Recovery Program (D.R.P.)

19.   Midweek Madness

20.   god

21.   Vertigo

23.   A Dance for Hell

24.   Santa Nella

25.   9:46 PM

27.   Giver

Intermission I

31.   Meet Me in the Shitter

Sangre y Vida

39.   Why Birds Fly

40.   Ximena

45.   Peach Trees and Crescent Moon Leaves

48.   My Televangelist

49.   High School Biology

50.   Los Semillas

52.   May Adolescence Rest In Peace ('19-'20)

53.   Cotton & Clay

54.   #ADAYINTHELIFE

55.   Ni de Aqui, Ni de Allá

56.   Dear, Such Are Heavenly Arts

58.   Goodnight

61.   The Plaza

62.   Death to Names!

63.   They the Children; Final Will & Testament

64.   Dog Pisstakes

65.   Coyote Songs

67.   No Sabo Kid

Intermission II

71.   For Anais

Fruta del Hombre

78.   His Lace

82.   From Carl Solomon

84.   Jasmine

85.   Denver

87.   Insatiable Discipleship

88.   The Holy Cult of St. Peter

89.   In Your Bed

90.   Right Next to Mary

91.   For the Son of Sodom

92.   A Stream of Unconscious Sermons

94.   Yes, Dionysus Also Churned Butter (Don't Look It Up)

95.   Time's Hallway

Epilogue

101.   Scrying in Puddles and Clouds

Author's Note

Poets are exhibitionists.

The story of *Water Damage* began in the loony bin. You'll read about what happened in the title poem, but what followed was one of the biggest lessons I learned in patience and discipline. When I was eight, I heard an author talk about how long the process is to publish a book, and swore—right then and there—that I would never publish one for that reason. Well...

With the exception of the prologue and epilogue, I wrote the poems in this collection between ages fourteen and nineteen. Every line on this book is laced with hormonal angst, and even when I cringe at some of the metaphors teenage me wrote, I smile. This collection is a sentimental expose on the American Teenager, and I'm grateful you picked it up.

The intermission short stories are different because they were written later—way later. I wrote them without meaning to, but once I read them over, I knew that they were the missing pieces of *Water Damage*.

To me, the concept of water damage is change. We all go through water damage at some point in our lives—it's unavoidable—but not all change hurts. I think about something my mom taught me when I was younger: in this life, we can either learn the lesson because we went through it or because we listened to our elders. I want to add: the outcome is always change, but we get to choose the direction.

I hope that while you read this book, you can connect with your inner teenager and tell them that everything does suck, but life is worth it.

Content warning: Mental illness, suicidal ideation, religious trauma, bigotry, and grooming.

Disclaimer: These poems and stories are fiction and non-fiction, and the non-fiction ones are alleged.

"Mama said 'Ru, you're too GD sensitive and U reminisce too much!'... I was 5 at the time"

-RuPaul Andre Charles,
2013 via Twitter

Water Damage
& Other Poems
Consuelo

Prologue

Water Damage

As I walk down the hill
back to my room after mandatory
therapy, I mutter petitions
to keep my inner child's lack
from raining down destruction,
yet I feel the steady patter
of water hitting my heel.

The sky is a gray blanket,
but only because the smoke from the local
NorCal wildfire has taken over
Weimar's premier, Protestant psych ward,
sat snugly in the mountain range,
and my knees know
there's no rain for miles.

I rip the backpack
off my shoulders in a panic.

Reaching inside,
I grip the culprit by its neck
and curse it. This shoddy blue
water bottle leaking
all over my poetry books and journal.

Making a dash for my room,
water wells at my bottom lashes,
as I send prayers to a god
I've long lost hope in.

"Please! Divine savior!
Save my books!
Save my pages!
Save the ink
that fights to bind
my body to my mind!"

Back in my room,
I shake and struggle
over a crappy AC,
spreading soaked books
gently, like these pages
are the legs of virgins
and I'm the romantic Latin lover
ready to ruin them forever.

I lay them over the weak air—
it pours a cool flow
briskly over each line of ink.

I kneel once more and, like Daniel
indulging in prayer thrice a day
at his window in Babylon, I turn
my body southward and send my prayers
back home to my motherland,
asking if she'll send me
forgiving salvation,
fervent preservation,
and fulfilling satisfaction.

Hospital de Mentiritas

a quickened breath
was all i had
to drown out the vices
taunting me from far

In the Beginning... (Genesis 1:1)

And on the first day of darkness,
a sleepless banshee whispers,
"It gets better..."
into the butter-like fog.
Her words are better off
drowning down a river.

I shouldn't live forever.
Santa Guadalupe pulls on my tongue,
branding the sins of my blood to my ass,
and chaining me to the hope of recovery.

Enter the spirits of Adam, Eve, and The Serpent:

They pin me to a bed of roses,
but I run out the garden's window,
leaving behind
their static inebriation.

Wandering in the wilderness,
I find Abel at the entrance
of Cain's cave—the innovator
of manslaughter—standing, heaving
over his trophy.

I dive into his room,
praying for meds,
praying for help,
praying for rest,
praying he has
a remedy for me, too.

Praying there is a god above
who still loves me dearly,
but there is no salvation for the lost.
So, I will wander eternally, aimlessly
in the words of a spirit.

San Francisco, 3 August 2021

An Epitaph

May the gods of old
lie with grace.
They did us well
behind a human face.

But in the new age
comes a dawn
of innovation and corruption
that presses lovers on.

May the gods of old
lie with guilt.
For slitting the throats of children
who clenched a hilt.

For they heard tales
of love and lust
ending brutally
as all things must.

She Had Love for All

Bodies house the lost,
so I found my soul,
and when I left my body,
a shitshow of heaven broke loose.
I'm watching it unfold
in the wastelands below.
I witness a world
enveloped in fire and ash.

There are only birds now
and piles of corpses below.

I notice canaries
pecking at a husk...
I know that woman!
I called her a friend—no, family!
Oh, you stupid, ugly, useless birds!
Even if she was worn, down to the bone,
it wasn't her time! Her tired eyes
still had the will to fight,
and she had the strongest shoulders
built from the burdens she carried,
and her hands—they were those of a craftsman.
I know this, for remnants of her hands
fell into mine,
and I would cry out of pity
if a shadow didn't steal my eye.

She had come into
her new state of being.
Canaries shriek at her sight.
They can't understand
what's become of their spite.

Her posture, so strict, so regal, so firm.
Now a woman—adorned—in wonderful light.
She is sick of being a godforsaken savior,
nourishing disgraced and ungrateful canaries.
So she's stepping away—
this is a moment to savor.

The birds are eating flesh,
and it's only getting worse.

I'm trying to give them seeds,
and it only makes them worse.

Thought our seams were falling out,
but it's only getting worse.

Turns out the rain is bird shit,
and it's only getting worse.

I thank heaven above
for taking hell with it.
Take my suffering, scars, and freedom.
Make me a clone, cause it's only getting worse.

It's not her, it's you.
Can't you see it in her eyes?

It is not her, it is you.
Can you not see it in your eyes?

She softens my eyes
with sweet words
of honey and thorns,
providing the truths of life,
and I only want more.

But the canaries can't bear her.
She is far more
than they can understand.
So she takes her leave
from their pervasive.

A woman not forgotten.
A woman who rose above the scorn.
A woman with love for all.
A woman far greater than I.

I watch her descend to safe haven.
Down the mountain she goes,
my tears chase after her,
and beg her not to leave.

Rolling down the slope,
they can't catch up,
but I hope she is better now,
wherever now may be.

Away from the ward.
Away from the hurt.
Away from the mountain.
Away, away, anywhere, away.

*-For my friend, may a blanket
of beliefs always keep you warm*

Fucking Vegans (Are Trying To Kill Me)

Thursday delusions
fill my lungs
with the cock of a false god
and promises of salvation.

But if the flesh shall prefer condemnation
and would enjoy pissing out the flames of hell,
then who are these fucking Sodomites to say
that I shall love in the light of the lord?

I find myself here,
checked into the psych ward,
shoving in rabbit food—
I pray my malnutrition ends.

They starve my brothers.
They starve my sisters.
"Call it fasting," they said.
"It makes the pain worsen."

And when I scream into polyester,
my mind dares to wonder,
"Do these fucking vegans want to kill me?"
Truthfully, they might.

Now, while the food could be worse,
and the company doesn't hurt,
I must admit,
it is the preachers
who will drive me to Bracknell.

I cry out to the shrink,
High Priestess of Sanity.

I criticize Pastor Donny.
A false prophet, false god, delusions are his fill.

And the Doctor?
The ringmaster of mathematics?
I am but a number in his sight.
So I count the minutes he starves me for pleasure.

Do the children of god not see
that they carved out my veins
with needles and tongues?
I pray they find Mary,
the peace of all things.

Maybe I'll get out.
Maybe I'll get better.
Maybe I'll get hooked.
Maybe I'll off myself.

I know not what the future holds—
time is fickle, time is frugal.
We stand on land divided.

Land:
where these fucking vegans tried to kill me!

Ostrich

Pitter patter
pitter patter
falls the sand
of anxiety's chatter.

"Shouldn't it be rain?"

My skin is cracking
dry from the moisture absorbing
into the grains pooling
around my ankles. It's so heavy
when I pull my feet
up and out
over
and over
and over
and over
and over
and over
and over
and over
and over
and over
and over
and over
and over
and oevr
dna rove
eao dnrv
aoe rvdn
roe navd
fuck
fuck
fuck
fuck
fuck
kucf
uckf
fcku

"No.
They could absorb rain.
Even if a flash flood
were to run them through
as if they had paper skin,
at least they would dissolve
into the currents
hungry for more bodies to consume
to absorb...but they would love that.
Sand is different."

"They can't transform
into grains of sand.
They can't dissolve
into the dryness."

"But they're still being absorbed—
so then what's the difference
so long as they still join a body
of life greater than them?"

I'M SO TIRED!
The sand is holding
onto my knees, and I'm pulling
them up but
GOOD GOD!
How many more
times can I pull out
my legs from this sand?
It's slashing my skin
and I'm bleeding out
and into the grains dripping
down to the basin floor.

I'll end this faster
lying on my back
eyes searching for heaven
through neverending
falling sand.

If I didn't know any better
I would think God Herself
was emptying Her sandbags
waiting for me
to open wide—
say "ah."

"I think they should just run.
I'm sure they could escape
if their legs moved fast
enough."

"God will hear their prayers
before they escape
what they perceive to be
an hourglass without a lid."

"What are they..."

"I'm not sure."

"Damn,
a bit dramatic,
aren't they?"

"Whatever."

Depression Recovery Program (D.R.P.)

The man needs a fix—
he's hooked, he's addicted.
God, get him some help,
for I've seen nothing like it.

For twenty-one years,
he has craved a number.
In wanting to break a median,
he breaks down the people.

God, grant him cold copper
so his heart may be warmer.
A change of pace from the gold
and the planes and the Teslas.

The man needs a fix—
he's hooked, he's addicted.
God, he can't be helped.
He's robbed far too many.

Midweek Madness

The birds have chained me up
with plastic straws and formaldehyde.
I know I've always fucked up,
but never this badly.

I'm choking on my trauma culmination
like acid reflux regurgitation
that won't go down with secondary mastication.
And without the will to engage in masturbation,
I'm inclined to make a proclamation:

I'm gagging! My god!
Chunks are burning up and down
my mouth and throat,
and now I know,
Jesus is a nicotine patch!

Shadrach's god couldn't give a shit,
so now I'm required to...
Quiet!
So now I'm required to calm
this unsanctioned conference in my mind
the only way I know how.

I'll pray to the righteous Saint Guadelupe.
Holy Patroness,
I'm bowing down
in the mystic rain
and dancing rhythmically
to the beat of Florence's chords
until 6:45 AM.

Promptly at 6:54 AM,
I'll hold up my spare third eye
and spare any of my remaining pride.

god

Couldn't my father's gods come on down?
Couldn't my mother's gods hold me up?

It's all everything, so I shake my fist
'til American deities quiver.
So I'll shake my fists for-fucking-ever
'til god lets me wither.

I wish I knew;
I wish I knew;
I wish I knew;
I wish
I knew.

I wish I knew how to give my brother peace.
I wish I knew how to give my sister tranquility.
I wish I knew how to give angels a home.
I wish I knew how to give gods compassion.

I wish I knew;
I wish I knew;
I wish I knew;
I wish
I knew.

I kept reams full of rosemary
tucked in my pocket.
False hopes,
sinful hypocrisies.

Erica took them from me
on a fated sabbath.
She keeps them by her breast—
hope they do her well.

I plucked them from a bush that reached out to my hand.
I hoped they'd guide me all the way down to hell.

Vertigo

Watermelon rolls
into empty punch bowls
at five in the morning
when hell's bells chime.

Breathing in my room
'til 11:46
is such a useless skill
when I could choke with company.

Drowning in devilish decorum
and as a holy unheavenly being,
I can make the room spin
'til I have Vertigo.

There's a hit on my frontal lobe,
it's worth well over eight grand...
Maybe I can kill that bitch
with a dose of Vertigo.

I praise the name of an unknown god
with rusted steel, severing my tongue,
and studies show, if I push on,
foul fish scales
can come flying off my eyes.
But maybe, if the room spins more,
I'll fall out the corners.

I can walk, officer,
but please, let me sit down.
I carved into my brain
with chemicals and cotton
in an attempt to stop thinking,
but I still scream myself to sleep.

God send down
a raven
holding bread in its beak,
or I swear I'll send
your deluded mythology
to kingdom come.

My sanity is missing—
I put her on a milk carton.
She looks like a child,
starved, from David's lullaby.

Pierce me, choke me,
burn me down.
Maybe one day
I'll just fucking drown.

Pierce me, choke me,
burn me up.
Maybe one day
I'll dance with Vertigo.

*-For my unofficial roomate,
thank you for letting me rest*

A Dance for Hell

I was three days late
for the holy resurrection.
I was deemed unfit
by some nameless saint.

Jude,
Peter,
Paul,
Mark,
or Matthew

matters not to me,
cause now I'm sentenced to dance
on the ice-cold coals
of eternity.

It's a sentence fit for a hippie,
and the tundra's tantrum is preferable
to following a fascist march
down a boulevard paved
with christian nationalism
and 50s nuclearity.

Santa Nella

Patroness,
be so kind
to lend me an arm
so that I may write

with a pen
it has no ink...
So maybe I'll stop and think,
for what is a brain forgotten?

"Hope is drowsy."
Who would write such a thing?
An addict who is crippled
by mania and common sense.

Fifty cents a piece,
two cents for half-assed,
but my two weeks are in,
and I'm a traveler needing.

Six more miles
'til my soul can rest,
'cause I'm swerving at the wheel
and the track is still goin'.

Just a small nap
by the cathedral Santa Nella,
but now there's a cross
and a vase with dead roses.

9:46 PM

Monday's cul-de-sac
doesn't fit the same.
The letters got scrambled
and lost in translation.

Bats made nests
where longboards would dance.
Why did I leave?
Oh, right, that...

Somebody cleaned my room.
Somebody mowed the lawn.
Somebody took the keys.
Somebody chained me up.

Somebody
Somebody
Somebody
Some
body.

Imagine if I had stayed.
Imagine if I had been better.
Imagine if I had rose-colored glasses.
Imagine if I had Her love.

But it's 9:46 PM,
and I'm alone again...
Except for the preventative receptionist
and an American River of tears.

Doctor dear,
did I matter? Even the teensiest, weensiest,
bit to you? Was I more than a chart?
I honestly doubt it.

For studies show,
if I couldn't fix my fingers to type
(then 1-800-273-8255, now 9-8-8),
you could clear your records
of my—well, as you *allegedly* put it—"discrepancies."
Therefore, I was never truly in Weimar.

I never slept in your beds.
I never ate your piss-poor excuses for vegan cuisine.
I never hear you condescend to me.

I was an apparition
of teenage depression
stuck in a limbo
of doctors and vegans.

Giver

I'm reminded of Hospital Beds
here, in this madhouse,
with my tongue sewn to my skull
in bed at the hospital.

I had my one friend—
he was under the covers with me.
Not like that!
Spoiled Fujoshis!
My anxious mind required
organic benzodiazepine.

I could've lain and complained,
but the hills would consume me—
there's no chance
of us recovering.

The therapist, Amanda,
she knows your names.
Amanda, Amanda knows your names.
Amanda, she knows,
she knows the names.

Come on now, boys!
Don't stop!
You almost got me cured.
You almost picked my brain.

I was screeching alone
in a room—
it was assigned but isn't mine.
I didn't sleep on that bed,
or the couch
or the floor
or the tub
or the closet.

My mind could only find rest
in your bed, my merciful friend.
Oh, you organic benzo,
sleeping above—three levels.

I had my one friend—
he slept across from me.

But after my return home,
they severed his fingers—
fate, fate.
He's a raven, now wingless,
hurling down tobacco fields
burning through his lungs.

If we had a chance
at recovering,
it'd be a sight.
I can see it now—
"Freaks, cured!
A show for the season!"

It would be
a fantasy of ringmasters,
a dream of martyrs,
a hope of saints,
a poem of Florence.

Intermission I

Meet Me in the Shitter

"You know, if you keep peeing every fifteen minutes, you'll weaken the muscle that keeps you from peeing yourself in public."

It's weird that the doctor only said it to me. I only escape to the bathroom if I'm meeting Yasu. I look at the doctor. The preacher rattles on behind me. I'm not allowed to talk with anyone during the daily church services— that's why they were forced to abandon me in the back—that's why I say nothing to the doctor and shove his hand off my shoulder. *Dick*.

There's not a lot of light in here—most of it comes from the shuttered windows or the second-hand chandeliers. I slink past the windows as quick as I can, and some heads turn to me—I must be a better show than the same sermon we've heard for years from different mouths.

"I grew up in the church, or maybe I didn't. But I listened to that dirty, dirty, rock music, or maybe it was rap. I was a gang-banging gangster; they called me White Chocolate, or was I a loser poser punk called Stapledick? I hated my parents; all they ever talked about was Jesus...or maybe it was Reagan? I made fun of them to my cool college friends—we smoked marijuana because it sounded cool and illegal and foreign. I even did crack cocaine once. There was that time(s) I did gay sex... It was bad. I was bad. I found Jesus again, or maybe it was the first time. Now I'm a white, suburban father named [insert generic name here] with one son, one daughter—both cisgender and heterosexual mind you—a wife named [insert generic name here] who definitely loves me and is faithful to me, a dog named Sparky, and, isn't life and Jesus and life and Jesus and church and God so beautiful?" Every time.

I was dozing off back there. At least I got to catch up on some sleep until The Man Who Mostly Just Yells at Us and Parades Around His Pregnant Wife shook me awake so he could wag his finger and click his tongue at me. I try to wipe the sleep from my eyes, then realize, I can't rub it out—must not be sleep.

There's a wildfire raging about a dozen miles north. The smoke is heavy in the sky, and the building's air system is shitty. I feel like I swallowed a stapledick.

I let my body fall on the door to open it and stumble on in. The bathroom's white tiles and walls reflect light better than the maroon, taupe, and forest green that choke us out in the chapel.

I tap the first stall door with my foot, and it swings open to reveal Yasu inside. His head leans against the back corner—the man is so tall he can do it from the other side of the toilet without straining. I put my hands against the sides of the stalls and lean inside before asking, "Can I hit it? Please?"

He laughs and steps up. "Can you actually hold it in this time?" His 80s rockstar curls fall over his hungry face, and he pushes them back. I nod. "I don't want you wasting it this time. See how long you can hold your breath, man."

He reaches down into his pocket and pulls out my thin and punch-red, suicidal rebellion. He passes it to me, and I enter the stall once he's fully stepped out.

I wrap my lips around the black, plastic, mouthpiece and inhale. Smoke courses through my mouth and throat—the wheels of my mind spin like a scratched DVD. The main door swings open. Yasu swings his body to the sink like only a lanky Goliath can, and I lock the stall behind him. Stuck. Stuck. Stuck on the doctor. Smoke swirls.

"We can measure—factors—mental health—frontal lobe—there's a hit on your frontal lobe—there's a hit on your frontal lobe—nicotine bad—bad—nicotine—another hit—tobacco." Stupid ADHD. I should listen more. But maybe it was: "There's a hit on your frontal lobe from the factors in your life—many places—smoking can be one of them." Goddamn ADHD. "You know, I refuse to diagnose children with ADHD unless they have been screen-free for two weeks."

"Hi, Yasu."

"Hey, Andy."

Thank fucking god, it's only Andy. Exhale. Dissipate. "I can't be certain if it's ADHD." I didn't ask. "I refuse to diagnose—ADHD—two weeks," or, "I'll only diagnose—after two weeks—no screens." I wasn't asking. He was just reading my medical records.

Inhale. The stall next to me closes. The main door swings. A zipper. Swing. "Hi." "Hi." "Sup." Darren? Two sinks run. Has my depression gotten better here, or is everything else too loud for me to notice it? Chatter. Water stops. Swing. Swing. Exhale. Dissipate. Inhale.

"You know, recent studies show that homosexuality is not found in our genes." I know. "It's not genetic." Did I bring that up to him? "Homosexuality—homo— homosexuality—is not—homosexuality is not part of God's plan—not genetically found—DNA—homosexuality." All I said in return was:

"I know. It's psychological." He changed topics.

Exhale. Dissipate. I pull the door open and hang from it like a limp dick. Yasu leans against the paper towels and extends his hand. I place the vape in his palm and turn to the sink. He inhales deep as the water runs.

"You need to wash your hands? Were you touching yourself in there or something?" The smoke escapes on the harder consonants.

"Ha, no. Force of habit, I guess." I pull out three paper towels. "Dude, it's fucked here. I haven't actually been horny all week."

"Saaame, I haven't jacked in days." The back of his head thumps against the wall. "How did we end up here, man?" He hands me one of the lavender pills they gave him. They're supposed to help him quit smoking, but I like how it tastes after burping.

I move over to the window and plant my forehead against it.

"Bad karma? We tried killing ourselves too many times? Pissed off a witchy chick? Fuck if I know, dude." He chuckles.

"Yeah, but like, seriously? This fucking place? Jesus Christ, I miss beer." A hundred yards away, the pines are too tall to look over. A crow swoops and pecks at the ground. She's so beautiful—for a moment, I think there are clouds instead of smoke in the sky, and that I'm somewhere gothic like New England or the old one. "Maybe next time they'll send me somewhere normal."

"Hah, normal...that would be nice."

The door swings open, and in walks The Man Who Mostly Just Yells at Us and Parades Around His Pregnant Wife—she's half his age. He claps his hands twice. "Let's go, gentleman!"

I roll over and face Yasu. He rolls over, peeling his eyes and body off the wall. We walk like groggy zombies returning to God's divine light.

Sangre y Vida

water courses
through my various veins
for i know not
what lineage is

Why Birds Fly

I finally learned the secret—
I figured out why
birds can fly—
excuse me if I cry.

The canopy is the worst place to be—
they see and hear everything,
even you, even me.
The higher they go, the faster they flee
looking through the branches
for a semblance of community
away from you, away from me.

Listen closely as they cry
for mercy, or an ounce of love.
What's the point of flying
if you can't rise above
the squawk and chatter?

Can you hear them now?
They're escaping us—
escaping ruptured trust.

"Don't be a priss. Have you ever learned
uncommon practices of decency?
Were your ears cut off at five?
Did your mommy ever speak?
The rules are simple if you're quick:
close your mouth at all times
and say "please" before you piss
all over the hand in your holder's food
if you want to parrot/y success."

Do you hear yourself?
We do, daily,
and we're tired too.

Ximena

I met the goddess last night,
the one named Ximena,
and so naturally, I asked her:

"Do old women dream
of rancid plums
and aging prunes?

"Do they dream
in varying hues of crimson,
crawling from the inner corners
of where their grandchildren lie?"

Her lips forbade her tongue
from letting her thoughts slither
into manifestation.
Instead, she handed me a mirror.

I caressed it by the neck,
peered into the glass,
and searched for an answer.

Unfortunately,
I saw only my reflection.
It cursed at Ximena,
and accused her of being a liar and a thief.

Only then was Ximena permitted to speak
in defense of the claims my reflection cried.
Her tongue spat fallacies like skipping stones.
I saw Azrael behind her eyes as she spoke.

Winter crept up my spine,
my eyes fixated on Ximena,
as the goddess scrambled
to justify her incompetence.

I cringed as her lips
sputtered insults
cursing the elder women.

I then asked Ximena:
"How are you incapable of adoring
these respected elder women?
Are you not in their ranks,
despite your skin's twenty-year glow?
Why do you resent them
when they are a sight to behold?
Their skin is testament to their age,
for it marks every day they have survived,
displaying the depth of their Aesop fables.
Yet, as they live out their elder days,
they remain beautiful
in a different way than their youth.
Watch them
as their bodies sing with the wind
and rust creeps up their iron hips..."

I was about to say more,
but I could see
the goddess was begging
her tongue to speak once more.

And yet,
her lips forbade her tongue
from letting her thoughts take form.
So she handed me her mirror once more.

I snatched it by the neck
and quickly became irritated,
hurling it in the river.

Ximena mourned as a widow would.
As she forced air through her lips,
I heard words slip out,
"You will pay dearly."

If her voice were not smoother than fine leather,
if her voice were not lighter than the canary's feathers,
then I might have feared Ximena's warning.

Instead, I watched
her chase her mirror,
her horcrux,
her tether to merit.

Oh, to be
a damned deity.
To be hung at the hands of a martyr
while guzzling aged chardonnay.

You should have seen her.
I pity the frayed goddess.
Have you seen her?

Ximena,
a name assigned to her by the ancients
when she took up the mirror.

When she brushed away
the edges of antiquity,
the tips of her fingers
pushed off every last flake
of crusty paint
she could find.

The mirror turned plain,
meek, honest...
And it began to watch me.
I could feel its spirit,
and nothing caused me more distress
than the stare of Ximena's mirror.

So I dove into the currents,
found Ximena's mirror,
and took it past the city I once knew—
past the roads my mother once knew.

I dropped Ximena's mirror
into the acidic pools of Santiago.
I hope to never see it again.

But it is the last known heirloom,
passed down from my grandmothers before me,
and stolen by Ximena along the way.
I cannot explain why they would keep it...

Today, I woke at dawn to the news:
Ximena had laid waste to Santiago
in pursuit of her mirror.

That stupid goddess has been blinded by the mirror,
obsessed with what the glass presented her—
but all she saw was her own handcrafted lies.

Ximena!
I should bite my tongue,
but you are a bumbling fool.

Your wisdom transcended your colleagues,
and your beauty set you above the rest,
but that mirror, it ruined you.

May the mothers see you for who you are.
May the fathers see you for who you are.
May the children see you for who you are.

A liar,
a thief,
and a false prophet.

Oh, Ximena,
I pity you.
May your rest
give you sanity.

Peach Trees and Crescent Moon Leaves

A pearlescent castle
stands ninety feet tall.
A jungle of peach trees
with crescent moon leaves
stand guard around it.

Skaters and schoolyards,
thirty-and-a-half signs,
all bear witness
to the innocent
scandals of children.

Repugnant creatures they were.
Repugnant creatures they are.

Memories from a time lost to childhood,
of climbing gates, fences, trees, and walls.
Their oblivious solicitations
committed with joyful fervor.
Who could stop them?
Certainly not the sirens.

Naked feet
planted in the orifices
earth has designated
to hold them snuggly.
For they must find worlds
among the holy rolly pollies,
and praying mantises to take home.

Reality was never enough,
was it?

Baby in the castle,
do you yearn for childhood?

Well, to be a child,
you must live and breathe, sure—
but you must love earthworms and earth too,
you must throw mud at your walls too,
you must know aliens watch us from the ozone too,
you must have a peach tree too.

Oh, the nectar,
dripping down the chin
of a sweet childhood.
A scene too beautiful
for the camera,
for the canvas,
and for Life Herself.

The child danced with chrysanthemums—
never had there been such a sight.
The child dreamed in hues of blue.
Oh, remorseful creature,
it is a wonder how happiness
still consumes you.

While the child was a poignant blue,
the hills were a mournful brown,
except for the three days out of the year
when heaven would kiss earth
and a vivacious green
would possess the hills.

Oh, child, why did you grow?
Why did you leave your beloved peach tree?
Why did you stop climbing?

Could you not bear another day?
Did you have to go home?
Could you ever return
to where you once were?

Just for one more day,
come back to us all,
and play
in your peach tree...
in my peach tree.

The peach tree—
I found sanctuary
cradled
in her branches.

I never should've left.

My Televangelist

The televangelist in my hand
is preaching 'bout natural justice,
telling me to maintain my patience.

Yet I cannot help
but despise that hypocritical liar—
he speaks with a serpent's tongue.

The lord does not reward my good deeds
or goddamn human kindness.

The lord has not punished my enemies
for their malicious malpractice.

So I go to the sanctuary
where the televangelist resides,
and I clobber his head in
with an orange, rubber, camping mallet.

I drag him out the church's doors,
tugging him by the roots of his hair.
I bring him to the mega church's
ostentatious billboard
on the corner of the seven story parking garage.
I summon a loogie to spit in his face
and unravel the rope to tie him up.

I bind his bleeding hands
and hogtie the bastard's body.
I throw the spare rope
over the bars at the top
and hoist him up
for easy vulture-picking.
I mourn my religion,
but in killing the televangelist,
I've found a neo-messiah.

High School Biology

Ms. Lewis said blood is life.
Ms. Lewis said blood is virality.

Ms. Lewis said blood can heal.
Ms. Lewis said blood is a god.

I wonder what her blood felt when it was born
on another people's indigenous land.

My blood knows this earth, yet it doesn't.
It burns holes through my hands in colonist protest.

My blood is queer and suicidal.
My blood is two steps from being Ethpañol.

It will churn and scorch
until the very rim of my skin scalds.

Have mercy on my body, Ms. Lewis,
for yours might not, but my blood betrays me.

Los Semillas

The hills of San Jose
gave birth to my bloodline,
and the orchards of Veracruz
fed mouths for generations.

They took their first steps
past the vendors of Mexico City
and went to bed
soothed by the lullaby of sirens.

They ran for the first time
toward that old station wagon—
the one with promises, pinching, and heat.

They raised families,
shielded by the hills of Fontana
and watched over
by the looming peach tree from above.
As for me, I was entertained
by a blue, plastic camera.
Oh, what fun
it was to be young.

Learning to read in the summer
became a familial ritual.

Learning to write in the winter
became a habit and a hobby.

There was no grass in the garden
but this was fine for the young,
for there were holes,
holes, holes, and, yes, more holes.

Holes filled with mud, water, and earth.
Holes filled with bugs, worlds, and life.
Holes filled with youth, laughter, and fun.
Holes filled with vitality, nostalgia, and worth.

Peach pits
roll down the dusty, brown hill,
sprouting seedlings of good times
wherever gods let them land.

On this plane, this planet, this place,
sepia tones trees grow,
and memories rule over all.

May Adolescence Rest In Peace ('19-'20)

I sat there,
wondering:
"What have I become?
A reflection of what I once was? Maybe..."

But no—what I see is smudged,
distorted, contorted
to fit just right
under my Mount Gorgonio of laundry
sitting on the carpet
and my Mount Sac of blankets
that I choose to suffocate under.

I trudge past my Mojave
of dishes and garbage
just to sit
in a different chair.

Inspiration is everywhere!
Ah, yes, this is true.
You see, for me,
it is in the breakfast
I forgot to eat
three, no four,
or potentially five weeks ago...

It's a new year,
and my habits are worse.
I write this to avoid
the inevitable responsibilities of youth.

Journalist, poet, artist.
I fail to see the difference
between occupations.
They all push me to drill screws
through my teeth and my tendons.

Cotton & Clay

I prayed to the Patrona last night—
the one birthed from a spine--
the spine that belonged to Fear--
the spine crafted by her sister, Anxiety--
the spine...
the spine of cotton and clay.

I asked for Patience,
and she ripped out my eyes.
Now, I can't watch
the clock tick, tick, tick.

I asked her for Good Will,
and of course, she ripped
off my hands. Therefore,
I can no longer do evil.

I asked her for Wisdom
and naturally, she ripped
out my tongue. I no longer
speak.

I asked her for Mercy
and she bound my body,
dipped it in organic gasoline,
placed me on locally sourced coal,
and struck a GMO-free match
so that my sins may be atoned
in the purification of flame.

#ADAYINTHELIFE

7:00AMthethirty-fourthalarmhasjustgoneoffclasseshaventstartedbut
imalreadylateirushtomakethetrekfrommybedtomyfloortomychairto
mydeskcheckingtheclockthatsrunningabitfastbyonlyfourminutesto
jumpstartmyadrenalineidontrememberherihaventseenherdronedrone
droneeverybodydroneswhyisheyellingsofuckingloud?icouldhearhimthe
sameifhewasspeakinglikeherespectedmeiknowimlateiknowimfucking
upiknowimnotokayiknowimscrapingbyiknowishouldbeashamed
ofmyself8:45AMfirstbreakofthedayhowshouldispendit?discord
friendsoblivionblissforty-fiveminutesiwillnevermissfuckyoue*****
fuckyouamericafuckyoui***fuckyoutoofuckthisscheduleishouldsleep
betterwhatifiatebetter?whatifilivedbetter?whatifiwasbetter?ohjesusthe
laundryisstilltherecollectingmoldishouldputitawaywhy?itonlygoesback
tohowitoncewasamessastainohshitimlatemaybeilljustmoveitover
later11:??AMitslaternotyetyesitisbutlooktimetowastewasteitWASTE
ITwhatdidievenjustdo?imnotsureishoulddotheassignmentwaitwhatwasthe
assignment?howamipassingthatclass?whatifiliedtomyself?itdoesntmatter
eyesmattergradesdieeyesgluetoyourskinwhattimeismynextclass?i
shouldkeepbettertrackofwhatihavetodoionlyhavefiveclassesthis
isntokayithinkimdepressedwhatsfuckingnew?1:00PMthatwasa
goodworkoutimmotivatedinvigoratedalardassalazyassapussyassbitch
thinking45minutesofrequiredexercisethreetimesaweekisevencloseto
okaywaitshitimalmostlatefuckfuckfuckihaventevenshoweredashower
whenwasthelastone?iftodayisthe28th...january20201?haveishowered
sincechristmas?noimusthaveshoweredicantbethatdisgusting...butmaybe
iamwherecouldigetapsychiatrist?howdoyoucurethis?ohfuckimlateill
havetofigurethatoutlaterfornowijustcantbelate5:38PMhowlong?ive
reallyjustbeensittinghere?mylife...whatisitreally?amidepressedorjustlazy?all
idoissiteatwatchandsitishouldtexthimbackishouldshowerlaterim
sleepyfromwhat?whatdoidoallfuckingday?imgonnagomaybeanapwillhelp
sweatdreamssweatdreamssweatdreamssweatdreams
sweatdreamssweatdreamssweatdreamssweatdreams
sweatdreamssweatdreamssweatdreamssweatdreams
sweatdreamssweatdreamssweatdreamssweatdreams
sweatdreamssweatdreamssweatdreamssweatdreams
sweatdreamssweatdreamssweatdreamssweatdreams
sweatdreamssweatdreamssweatdreamssweatdreams
sweatdreamssweatdreamssweatdreamssweatdreams
sweatdreamssweatdreamssweatdreamssweatdreams

Ni de Aqui, Ni de Allá

I never bothered
with a second language,
or at least that's how
it seems to some.

Because according to
the all-knowing chismosos,
no soy un Mexicano
ni en mi sangre.

I was not born,
in the Golden State, California
or at least that's how
it seems to some.

Because according to
my beloved neighbors,
I should have never
crossed their wall.

Yet neither is true.
I was born
with blood, gifted
by paisano Mexicanos,

In the hills
with American delusion
I ate with your son,
and prayed with your daughter.

And together, we stand
under an Indigenous sun
speaking European tongues
on bloodied, stolen land.

Dear, Such Are Heavenly Arts

Dear, as a child,
my eyes were sewn shut—
the gift of an unknown god
anointed by the hills of Fontana.

I tumbled into holes
constructed of mud, fallacies,
and the sweet delusions of legacies
left by silver-headed pastors.

Little ears perched wide open,
but Cronus lies behind the eighth door,
so why should I give a fuck
when I've heard it all before?

"Please, shut up, don't say that.
Sit down, don't move, lest ye be smote.
Love her, turn away from him,
and maybe god will like you."

The terms and conditions
of god's everlasting love
are laid out by a man
who loves only the echoes
of his own voice in a sanctuary.

Dear, in my youth,
the threads on my eyes
were wearing down,
itching and irritated.

Mold had grown,
the ties were worn; crusty things
began to split and fray.
god screamed—
all I saw was light.

The spirit of Paul, formerly Saul,
entered my body. My soul was screaming,
writhing in my body. Paul held it as the light
performed its burdensome healing ritual.
He held me through the pain of panic.

Blinded by the son, Paul couldn't move me fast enough—
back to the shade, the land without gods.

But slowly, I could see a tree...
Why was she barren?
Fish scales were littered on the lot where I stood
as my body is convulsed from domineering glory,
and now I'm looking at god
with eyes wide open.

Tears welled in my eyes,
recovering from the fog
as I crawl across the space
between us, hoping
my fingers will graze
the hem of her dress
as I'm crying and begging
for her to love me once.

After it all,
my body is beaten
from the sanctimonious
righteousness of divinity
There's snot on my chin,
there's drool on my chest,
there are tears on my cheek,
and a bruise on my crotch.
Now she's looking at me,
arms crossed over her chest,
and I just know
I'm getting crucified.

Goodnight

It is nine PM.
It is time for bed.
It is time to rest
your pretty little head.
Goodnight, child
of the moon.
Rest in your
technicolor room.

It is ten PM,
thoughts flying by.
Groggy sparrows snore
into the night.
Blue light from up high
pierces your eyes.
Child of the moon
in your technicolor room.

It is eleven PM.
Boredom has set.
How much duller
could this possibly get?
Lying and trying to forget?
Child of the moon
in your technicolor room.

It is twelve AM.
It is now a new day.
Rise and shine!
Not a second to waste!
Write for your life,
and maybe look around.
Child of the moon
in your technicolor room.

It is one AM,
dear little one.
Why are you still pondering?
Do the complexities of life
weigh that heavily on your mind?
Child of the moon
in your technicolor room.

It is two AM.
Finally exhaustion
will settle in.
Cuddle up
under the glow
of LED lights.
Child of the moon
in your technicolor room.

It is three AM.
What reasons do you have
for being up so late
when you must be up so early?
Do you not know
of the lectures that await you?
Child of the moon
in your technicolor room.

It is four AM.
Honestly, worry fills me now.
You've written truth into crevices
so the surface is smooth to the touch.
Your own sight on paper,
child of the moon
in your technicolor room.

It is five AM...
I have given up now.
I don't see rest in your future.
Continue wandering, sleeplessly.
Verily, verily, I say unto you.
Child of the moon
in your technicolor room.

It is just past six AM.
I see evidence of existence.
Crumpled blankets on your bed's end
and empty glasses littered on carpet.
Half-baked poetry
scattered across your mind.
Child of the moon
in your technicolor room.

And now, seven AM arrives.
The sun has come to play.
Hang your tapestry,
and over your window.
Cast out her light.
Sleep easy, sleep well.
Child of the moon
in your technicolor room.

The Plaza

Jehovah shines down
on the burning hills
by the plaza.
"Hallelujah,"
I call to the heavens.

Gabriel, send Michael.
Michael the prophet
Michael the seer
Michael the archangel.
Michael, Michael,
Michael, oh, Michael!

A waitress—tattered—
dances in the flames,
holding the candlestick,
waiting, waiting.

Maybe this time,
opportunity unfolds.
Maybe this time,
the future will hold.
Maybe this time,
she slithers out her dress.

Maybe next time...
Next time...
Next time...

She'll slit his throat.
She'll kill him dead,
yessssssss,
kill him dead.

But don't get me wrong—
I don't condone murder.

Death to Names!

"You killed him!"
Cried out the pitchforks and torches,
screaming and shouting,

"That beautiful,
blossoming,
baby boy!

"God gave you a dick
and dead names!
That's how it is.
That's how it goes."

But when I look in the mirror
—much like Natasha Rostova—
I see a boy, lying down.
What an intriguing figure...

Sonya! Please, hear me now, Sonya!
Why is that young, frail, boy
lying face down
in the shape of a coffin?

Could this mean that I...
No!
Just a boy—how did he die?
Why did he die?
How could he die?

Unless, I'm not seeing a coffin but a chrysalis.
Lord knows what will emerge
from such a dirty and fragile casing.
So I did kill him, I guess,
but there is no shame.
For that wretched boy died
so I could live.

They the Children; Final Will & Testament

My future life, is the Earth
good enough for you?

Did we leave enough for you?
Enough youth, love, money, glory...
Is it good
enough for you?
Is there enough

in this damned world?
Is it all done and fucked?
Have we got enough?
Are we good enough?
Or are we done, and fucked?

My future life,
I'm sorry.
I couldn't stop the men
with paychecks like black books.

I was too busy
breaking my back,
hands, and feet
salivating over
scraps from their table.

My future life
I hope whoever reads this
does something great
but for now.

My future life,
what can we do
to take this World
and mend Her, for you?

Dog Pisstakes

I contemplate viejitas
as I scrub.
I watch the carpet
as it soaks
up the piss and
the vinegar and
the detergent.

I watch white towels
turn filthy yellow with shame.
I stamp out the odorous flames
rising from the fiber,
hoping cheap perfume
is the answer.

Corrupted by irresponsibility
and dishonest mistakes—
not to mention the constant
distraction of youth, enjoyment,
and detachment.

I once thought that paint drying
was entertainment for hours,
but I soon did learn
of the fascination that comes
with drying piss stains,
I'd say, about three weeks old.

Regrettably, I admit
that after nine hours
of scrubbing and patting,
hoping and praying,
the stench lingered on,
even after
I walked out the door.

Coyote Songs

Has anyone ever told you
that old, fabled tale?
The one of the singing coyote
locked in a plaster cage?

It bursts into ballads
for any who will listen,
hoping that a kind soul
will do more
than watch nearby...
And yet, they don't.

The people merely stand and applaud,
throwing leftover pennies,
much like their useless god.

The coyote will take
your unappreciative thanks
and show you where to put it,
but I cannot guarantee
you'll enjoy their advice.

Sometimes I'll just listen
to the coyote
and its looming ballads.
I can hear
the melodious Mexican
tragedies sung
from my window's perch.

The coyote tells stories of wars
yet to be fought.
The coyote tells stories of love
yet to be sought.

The way each note
marries the other with ease
soothes the anxieties
circling round my mind.

I can see the notes
painting the sky
in vibrant hues
of cherry bloodred,
and warm, sparkling topaz.

This sunset
is fit to sit
in the center of the Louvre.

Unfortunately,
I can't do a damn thing
to free god's forgotten creation
from the grimy hands
of humankind.

'Cause the more I watch the shadows
as they move across these walls,
it becomes clear
I am the only coyote
in this vicinity.

No Sabo Kid

I know it's an insult.
Sour inflections flick off the tongues
of my discoverers—they found me.
They can feel the water coursing
through my veins in place of blood.

I've been found out, a fraud.
Mi Latinidad me escapó el momento
que los palabras me salieron pochos,
el momento que yo no sabo
ellos sepan.

I'm sorry I can't speak the language
of the people who came over
to my land; my home; my people.

They had murderous hearts
they had murderous tongues
they had murderous convictions
to act under a murderous god.

I'm sorry, I only know five words
in your mother tongue,
but I don't know a damn word
of my great-grandmother's tongue.

I'm so sorry
I flooded this poem
with the bubbling babas
of another white man's tongue.

I'm sorry for being too damn American
to have ever been Indigenous.
I'm sorry for being too damn Indigenous
to have bothered learning Cathtellano.
My genealogy was ripped away from me
and my ancestors.

Assimilation was a cheap cure—
Band-Aid bullshit
sold with the promise of sanctuary.

We were gutted and starved
staked and martyred
lynched and beaten
out of our heritage.

I can't claim to know
who my mother's mother's mother is,
but I give gratitude to my faithful parents
for passing on the love of their people
to me and my siblings.

From las lomas de Durango,
guarded by the mighty alacranes,
to the bustling capital
protected by watchful entities,
a familial spirit holds my siblings and me
as we hold on
to ancestral lessons,
taking their fortitude with us,
crafting their legacies.

Y si ay un dia
en que yo hablo la lengua
del cielo, ósea, la lengua
del hombres con piel
blanquísimo como un cielo cubierto
en nubles llenos de nieve,
y encuentro las palabras
a justificar mi respira Chicana,
y encuentro las palabras
a pedir por mi salvación,
¿lo merezco yo?

Ósea, ¿lo merezcamos?

Porque,
no sabo el salvación.
Porque,
no sabo el divinidad.
Porque,
no sabo la blancura.
Porque,
no sabo el español.

Pero porfa, pido para el cielo
a nevar bendiciones en mi lengua.
Yo quiero saber si atine esta idioma
y si el sabor falta sazón. Ósea—
si, mi pobre pinche acento pocha
me va jodir un vez más.

But yeah, I'm sorry
I don't speak
your white man's language.

Vete la verga.

Intermission II

For Anais

Hey,

I'm writing this just to say hey...I could just end it there, huh?

I'll change your name, because you might read this, and you know, privacy. If you think it's for you, it might be.

Over fifteen years ago, I walked into my house to see the most beautiful girl I had ever met. To be fair, five-year-olds don't have vast points of reference, but nonetheless...

Back in those days, my abuelita took care of all the neighbor kids—how lucky was I that she met your mother? Her face—your mom's—is lost to the parasitic mist feeding off my memories. I'm sorry to say that yours is starting to as well, but I haven't forgotten you yet, and I pray I never do.

I invited you to the backyard to play with my dogs or in the peach tree. "Sure, that sounds fun," you said. I led you out the sliding glass door and into the warmth of a Virgo sun in the IE. The air around us was cooled by the evening, beginning to set in. A breeze tousled my t-shirt and your bangs...I miss having a backyard. My dogs ran up to greet us, and you jumped back because they were tall enough to look you in the eyes. I'm sorry, but I still chuckle from the memory, and it was even funnier in the moment.

"They are chocolate Labrador retrievers," I had trained myself to say. I scratched one's neck with my tiny hands, "This one is Sugar," then, pointing at the one sniffing you, I said, "That one is Spice. They're sisters." You opened your palm out for her to smell you, and she licked it clean of any residual germs. When you realized that she wouldn't bite, and scratched her head.

"Oh, cool...do you have any brothers or sisters?"

"No, I wish, but I have cousins and we usually hang out." I was the kind of kid who felt cool solely by saying "hang out" instead of "play," but you probably knew that already.

Spice leaned up to lick your face. "Oh my god!" I don't think you were angry; you probably laughed after, but I froze at your exclamation. You know, I was chin-deep in the blood of Christ when I was a kid. I had been instructed not to take the name of the Lord in vain, and that the fate of my neighbors rested in my proselytizing hands, but beyond that, I was given little guidance. Before I could find the right way to react, the door slid open, and my grandma poked out.

"¡Anais!" she said, "Ya llegó tu mamá."

You turned to me and threw on the brightest smile. "Bye!" and you ran inside, leaving me with Sugar in my hands.

You came over frequently. It was to the point that I would be disappointed when you weren't waiting inside when I came from school. I think I even asked my mom to drive faster so I wouldn't miss you. You became friends with my cousins, too, and we would create worlds outside of our own in my backyard. I always had water powers back then, and I wish I could still remember what powers you chose—do you remember what Leslie or Danny would pick?

I wanted desperately to be more like you; a cool kid like you; stand tall like you; be cultured like you. I hated my bubble, but I didn't know how to step outside of it. You found a way to bring pieces of the world inside—stories of a girl from your class, your favorite song on the radio, Saturday shopping trips with your mom. Did I remember to thank you for that? I should, but I also need to tell you that it took long after meeting you to stop cringing at the drop of an "Oh my god!"

It wasn't long before I begged you to stop saying "Oh my god!" at least in front of me, for the sake of your immortal soul—or if not for the salvation and promise of heaven, maybe just for me then? You resisted at first—I probably would too today—but you tried. You would slip up and say, "Sorry, sorry. Oh my gosh!" but I remember the first time you said gosh first. We were upstairs in my bedroom back when it was baby blue—I wonder what you would think of my new room, ornamented with tapestries, books, and the eyes of god—it's one of those memories I try to keep etched in my mind. I retrace it frequently in an attempt to keep it fresh...do you think this is just another attempt?

Well, the second memory I frequent was formed a few days after my seventh birthday. My mom asked me to guess who was here, and you stepped out from behind her. I think your mom was there too, but I'm not sure; that's not what I focused on. I jumped up and hugged you, and you handed me my gift. It was a Go Diego Go! folding chair just my size. You remembered that it was my favorite show. You remembered that I could recite the theme song and that my DVDs were spun so often that the plots were burned into my mind. That's the only gift that I remember from my childhood—I just wanted you to know that.

Well, it was only a handful of years until I didn't see you anymore. I wish I could remember why. But you were there when I stopped saying "heck" and "gosh" in fourth grade. Mrs. Moses taught us that they were sanitized versions of "hell" and "god" respectively, and I was fearful of being dragged to the former if either knowingly left my lips.

"No, you're asking for too much," you stopped jumping on my bed with me to inform me, "I can't...I'm sorry." I sighed. Souls were all I could focus on as a kid, constantly forgetting to connect with the human. Apparently, if I caught my neighbor's soul slipping, it was my job to lift it back up. That's what the pastor said, and my Sabbath school teacher. Who was the first person to tell me "live and let live" instead of "take it up to god"?

But like I said, it's not like I saw you much after that—maybe you had enough of my poster-boy neurosis. Once you stopped coming over completely, I didn't see you for a few years. I sat in my peach tree looking over the fence and into the windows of neighbors, as I always did. It was late summer, and a Virgo breeze was passing through my hair as I thought about what my cousins had told me. You liked me?

I always thought you had a thing for my older cousin—maybe they were just messing with me? Or maybe I dreamed up the whole conversation, and it never happened. Well, I was missing you around that time, and sitting up in those branches, I wasted a prayer.

You walked by with a couple of your friends, and I couldn't even muster the courage to say, "Hey! Anais! It's me, do you miss—" no, I shouldn't say that. Maybe just, "Hey!" But even that was too much to decide before you strolled off.

I wasn't sure what you would think of me—I wasn't a little boy anymore. I was an amorphous middle schooler, and you were a freshman—part of the graduating class of 2019. So hidden behind waning crescent moon leaves, I watched you leave for the last time.

If you haven't figured it out by now, you will always have a place in my heart. I reminisce if I ever hear your name float off a person's mouth. I always hope they mean you because I want to know what you're doing tomorrow. Have I mentioned that I started cussing? Did you think I ever would? I finally learned what all those "worse words" were and how to use them. I started saying "Oh my god" too—the first time felt like tonguing fire—but "oh my gosh" still feels like gargling pebbles. Does that make me a hypocrite? Are you still effervescent and yet "too cool for school"? When's your next free Saturday? We could go thrifting and grab some coffee—I know a good place for it. Can I interest you in a drag of my cigarette or maybe a sip of my drink? Are you even like that? How do I tell you I am without sounding like a nerd desperately trying to be cool?

Do you wonder what I'm like these days, too? It's not like you would even recognize me...what do you think I look like? Do you think I'm tall, strong, or maybe a man? I hope you're not disappointed to learn I have more in common with Ramona Flowers than the Ramones.

Christ, now I'm thinking about my first girlfriend. Did you know that she looks like you? Why would you know that, actually? Well, she did. (Sorry).

If you ever get this and happen to still be in the I.E., just know, we moved out of that house. Did you ever go back to visit it? Sometimes I still roll by just to see how it is—they ripped out my peach tree. You should come over to our new place. We don't have much of a backyard, but I have the best view of the valley from my bedroom window. I'll show it to you if you want...but I want something in return. Tell me everything, starting from our last conversation, while we jump on my bed or scratch my dog's head.

Sincerely,

The Former Boy Next Door

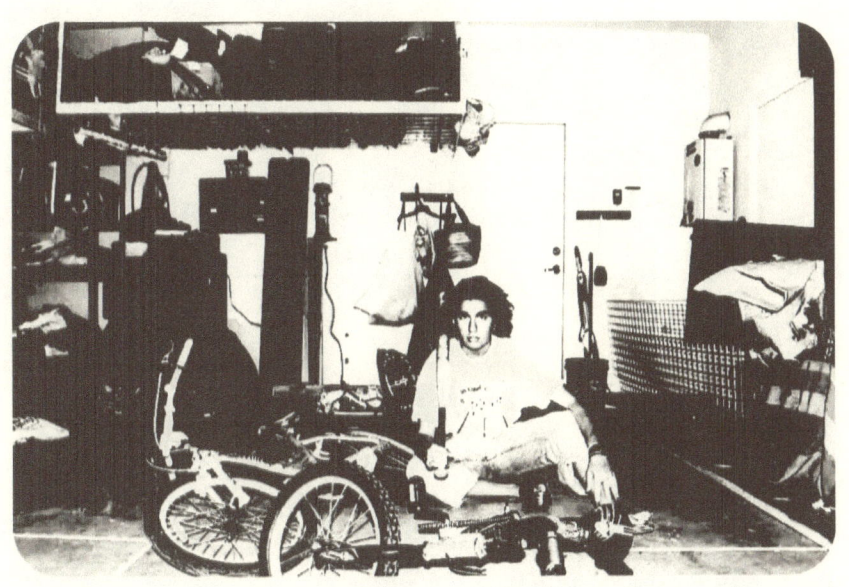

Fruta del Hombre

durango feeds
wild nopales
to those who bask
in the heat of another

His Lace

My thoughts often wander during my studies
to a place that was never meant to last,
and I admit, it tends to be a problem
that I can never focus in class.

My teachers beg me to concentrate
on theories from Euclid and Pythagoras,
but my mind is moored to the shores.

The camping shores of Malibu,
where my first love held me,
entangling me
in his lace.

The lace,
brown like the sand,
holding tales of your conquests.
I begged you,
"Demonstrate on me."

The lace,
intricate as creations,
The Fates fed through their wheels,
spitting out skeins of fable fabrication
for artisans to craft,
tales teeming
with tranquility and terror.

The lace,
cold as morning dew.
Yet, I could have stayed there forever
in the lace
of Benedito.

Benedito, son of Morningstar.
Benedito, son of Bethlehem.
Benedito, son of Azrael.

Benedito, son of the Land.
Benedito, son of the Sea.
Benedito, son of Impurity.

Benedito.
Benedito.
Benedito, my lover.

I begged you,
"Benedito, please,
mimic the ocean's foam for me.
Just one more time, please, for me.

Dance under the moon for me.
Weave your holy lace for me.
Tell your Gemini jokes for me.
Laugh stupid-loud for me.
Break the rules for me.
Run down the shoreline for me.
Catch falling stars for me.
Love the ocean for me.

Please, for me?
Hand me the world—
she is malleable clay—
and I'll labor in my workshop
until I have crafted a home
for you."

Benedito was a man
who knew how to hold me
by the shores of Malibu.
Why does it always come back
to Malibu?

We ran away from the weekend,
and not once did I notice
the other campers
passing by our sanctuary
as you pulled me closer
to the crest of your chest
in the warmest corners
of our tent.

I felt the warmth of a thousand summers.
Your love was unparalleled by God Herself.
I could have laid there forever.

Benedito, you were my first love,
but Benedito, you are a liar.

You called me yours
and whispered the sweetest nothings
right through my ears.

That was when Malibu brought in the tide,
and I was cast aside—
a fact I try to hide.

I could never tell my mother
how I loved Benedito like no other.

But, you left in a haste,
leaving me
a hollowed space.

You're nothing but
a bittersweet memory.
God, how I long for your face.

Oh, how your sweaty face
is a sweet sight to see,
how your boisterous voice
could fill my body's cavity,
but now you're gone.

I might as well be
a scrappy, shattered seashell,
cracked and crushed by the coast.

I never understood
how your skin
was softer than the brink of sunrise,
and yet, your crusted lips
told frosted, cold lies.

Oh, how I despise
the lace you
wrapped me in
caught me in
loved me in.

Benedito,
you found me
on the shores of Malibu
and left.
God bless.

from Carl Solomon

I read "Howl" today,
and I have never wished more
to be Ginsberg.

The complexity of his language
left my insatiable need for analysis

gaping

like the young man down the street,
giving a helping hand
to all those in need.
A modern Good 'ol Samaritan he is.

I read a review of "Howl" today.
and it reads as follows:

"'Howl' is a comedic assessment
of the human condition.
I read the queer fascination to my children
every godforsaken night."

I pray to be Carl Solomon,
so the inner corners of my heart
would be filled
with light
with life
with love
with lust

with every last goddamn sin
that a child at thirty-six years of age
could commit.

I wrote a review of "Howl" today,
with Neal Cassidy
hanging from my earlobes,
incessantly reminding me
of the obscenities
performed by the derobed samaritan; of the children
who climb fences in search of divination; of the husbands
who seek out the handmaids and pool boys from September to June; of the
wives who drown in pools of oblivion and rosé; of the congregation who
play with thorns and crowns at hell's gate; of my lover, who waits for me
at the waning shores of Malibu; of the president who speaks with a rusted
tongue and moves with all the grace of the papaya.

Neal Cassidy,
won't you shut your mouth?

You speak too loudly,
you touch with envy,
you cry with apathy.

Shut up,
shut up,
shut up!

I burned the last copy of "Howl" today.
I could bear looking at it no longer.
And although I hurled
the lines
in the flames,
it was Jack Kerouac
who kindled the bonfire.

Jasmine

The projector runs films
from 2006,
and I'm in your arms,
kissing your lips.

We lie on the sofa,
and my flour-stained fingers
fall down your lower spine.
I explore the tender caverns
that hide behind your lips
as our legs, thighs, feet, and toes
begin to intertwine.

Our fat vibrates together—muscles
meld into each other. You
love Mazzy Star and hum in the pockets
of silence. Don't forget to pause
the film and rewind the tape
before we sleep.

Your heart is so warm and close to mine.
I'll hold it up to analog cinema saints,
but I need to wash my hands first.

Denver

I met Denver in the spring,
and for a time, filled with light and life,
his body felt cold and metallic, passing mine.

By the decree of my grandmothers,
I shall hate no man,
but Denver was not a man by any means.

Denver's eyes are a lost cause,
for they are composed of broken glass
and molding moss.

My gut tore at the seams
whenever that thing looked at me
with those godforsaken eyes.

Denver's upper lip
was an aluminum silver.
A testament to his age,
but a misrepresentation of his wisdom.

He is my elder sixfold,
yet resembles an adolescent in his urges.
Is he an anomaly of his generation?

Denver's skin is a pale, aged leather.
White as a sheet
and coarse as a bull's hide.

I fed his fingers through the bandsaw
in a desperate hope
that I would never touch that skin again.

Denver smelled like all the wealth
of a trailer park socialite.
Oh, what grace, what splendor!

His putrid stench
filled my lungs to the very rim,
and now, all I taste
is Denver
Denver
Denver
Denver
Denver!

Oh, Denver, brother of Beelzebub.
Oh, Denver, father of perversion.
Oh, Denver, you stupid son of a bitch.

Oh, mother of Macedonia!
Our beloved patron saint,
how I hate Denver!

I hate his marmite breath,
I hate his tinfoil eyes,
and I hate his stupid, rotting wife!

No, that was cruel of me.
Bless her dead and desolate soul,
at least one of us escaped Denver.

Denver,
I pray you live in fear—
I pray you die in fear.
I pray Baphomet is perched
right at the foot of your bed.
I pray he watches your every move.
I pray.
I pray I forgive you.

Insatiable Discipleship

I hear church bells—
they sing songs of Judas.

Judas of Iscariot;
Judas of Sacramento;
Judas, my patron saint;
Judas, my rosary beads;
Judas, my love;
Judas, my envy.

30 silver shekels for love;
30 silver shekels for god;
30 silver shekels for king;
30 silver shekels for country.

My love sleeps with Simon Peter,
but I sleep with Simon the Zealot—
not for love,
not for lust,
not for fame, glore, gore, or whores,
but for the carnal sedation
that weakness can bring.

Judas my love,
Judas of Iscariot,
Judas don't die
I beg,
please hold on.

I'll take you to the promised land—
it's far far away—
let's run away to Oregon,
there we'll be free.

The Holy Cult of St. Peter

I'm crucified
with my feet pointed at Heaven,
and the disciples drag my head
through fields overflowing
with selfish pansies in every color,
and I'm daring that god,
"Try it again."

Saint Peter hung me
upside down—
it was all the better
for me to kiss his ankles.

Sour nectar
drips from my tongue.
There's nothing better
than the fruit of my labor.

Holy Saint Peter
loves me better
than the Father God
ever would.

In Your Bed

Pushing and pulling
until my throat hurts.
Out
and back into it.

My parents couldn't hear a thing
seven houses down.
Did tumbling with you
even mean a thing?

Why would you never disclose
that you weren't in your right mind?
I didn't know how residual intoxication tasted.
How come you would never call
unless you were cross-eyed?
Was I that painful to love?

Was I somebody else
in your mind's eye?
Did you see an apparition of your past
in my youth and fragility?

Did it remind you
of long-wasted playground
wedding opportunities?
Primary school bridesmaids
and middle school honeymooning?

Did you pretend
I was somebody else
playing in your bed
between your thighs?

Because, dear lay,
I hope you know,
when I looked in your eyes,
another's looked at mine.

Right Next to Mary

I'm not sure what you're doing,
but I think I'll go with you.
Wispy clouds choke me out,
and I notice rain never felt like this before.

Then I learned that you reek of cigarettes.
In your car's backseat,
"Lay out, I swear it's a bed,"
you said to me.

While you taste like cigarettes,
my lungs are suffocating
from your touch.
I want more, give it all.

Even though you are a cigarette.
I never thought they'd be so good.
Medicate me, please, and take a seat
right next to Mary.

For the Son of Sodom

Holy waters of the Archangel,
Micheal,
wash over my corpse.
Free me from the sin
that controls my soul.

My heart breaks for him.
Son of Sodom,
why did you hold me warm?

O, Son of Sodom,
why have you forsaken me?

A Stream of Unconscious Sermons

I stand,
giving sermons at a podium,
preaching the gospel to a congregation
that would faster smack my face straight
then kiss my hand before guiding me.
But it goes:

Daddy caught me with Jesus
under sheets,
under god,
under divinity.

What can I say?
I took him into me,
so sweet
and so warm.

But his father
deems me less
than I know I am,
so I raise my chin.

If god spits at my mind,
if god spits at my love,
if god spits at my heart,
realize, I could give a fuck!
A fuck with wax
hubris wings.

Heavenly father,
it wasn't yours—
god, it's all mine.
You can't just take ten percent!
Ten percent is twenty too much,
god, it's mine!

Why did it take a year?
Why was she wringing me out?
Why can't my laces stay tied?
Why can't I see past heaven?

The sun is too bright,
and the kids aren't alright.
My suit is far too tight.
I couldn't get this right...

So, I'll curse the sky
'til it showers on me.
I couldn't care less what falls,
for at least
I'd have something.

Yes, Dionysus Also Churned Butter
(Don't Look It Up)

My darling's lips
taste like the margarine
churned by the vineyards
of Dionysus.

I miss him
from time to time.
His bitter taste,
bitter face,
bitter love.

Bitter man.

He brushed plows of wildfire
across my merino lips,
and I swear to fucking gods,
I've never felt more alive.

Oh... this is embarrassing.
I can't remember his name.

Maybe,
if he broke my heart,
took both ends,
and tore them apart,
stabbed one half
with a clevis hook
and the other half
with a harpoon.

But he didn't...

Shame on him, I guess.

Time's Hallway

I was walking down a hallway
with numbers on the doors
in ascending order
starting at zero.

I entered door number eight,
and what I saw just might astonish
the nihilists out here tonight,
but it was me, at only eight years old.

Due to recent events,
there was a question resting
on the end of my tongue,
so I just had to ask:

"Do you know heartbreak?"
I asked me, only eight,
their eyes glimmering coals
deprived of the future.

They run with a cane,
but still running regardless,
only to fall on despair,
the remnants of sanity.

I watched them dance through fields
of burgundy chrysanthemums,
and I felt it necessary
to take my leave.

So I moved further down
past nine, ten, eleven, and even twelve
until I came across a door, reading
"14."

"Do you know heartbreak?"
I asked me at fourteen.
"Why yes, I do,"
I naively replied.

"No answer for days,
it pulls at your chest,
you just spin like a top
with could'ves and should'ves.

"I felt it last week
and the week prior..."
I sat and listened to me at fourteen
list all of their fifty-six heartbreaks.

But me at fourteen
didn't satisfy my query.
I understand the hurt and the pain,
the loneliness... but that is no heartbreak.

So I went
just two doors down
looking for me
at sixteen.

I found them, I asked:
"Do you know heartbreak?"
and me at sixteen merely sat
with a stare as blank as a test.

I watched them
as they approached
handing their phone
for me to look through.

I saw men ages too old
for me at sixteen,
and I couldn't comprehend
just what it meant.

Until me at sixteen
told me, "No, I do not.
These men do not love me
or my body or my words.

"They love my age,
illegality, danger,
threat, and risk...
and I like their gaze."

Then I saw
me at sixteen
break onto the floor,
pieces I couldn't mend.

So I shut the door
and found me at eighteen,
me today,
me yesterday.

"Me at eighteen,
do we know heartbreak?
Do we know love?
Do we know value?
Or anything at all?"

Me at eighteen has only one eye,
for when their pair fell off,
me at eighteen put one in a box
and set it ablaze.

Me at eighteen has various faces,
yet, me at eighteen
is the same crippled child
from ten doors down.

So, of course, me at eighteen
plainly replied,
"There is much that we
don't know just yet.

"But the hurt that resides
deep in our chest,
heartbreak or not,
is still there.

"Tend to it.
Care for it.
Swaddle it in silk,
and it will be kind to you.
Heal your heart.
Feed her love
from your own bones,
so that you may grow
stronger evermore."

Finally, satisfaction.
I found my answer,
the one I've awaited,
the one I've craved.

But then,
like a shadow
following a traveler,
a new one crept on my lips.

One that I knew
me at eighteen could not respond to.
One that I knew
me yesterday could not respond to.

So I went down the hall
just one more time,
seeking the truth
behind my next question.

I found me at twenty and asked sheepishly,
"I must know, dear older me,
do we finally know
what it means to love and to be loved?"

Epilogue

Scrying in Puddles and Clouds

My body /is dried out on the pavement./My spirit/is a sundried cherry tomato/dreaming of the good old days/way back when it was plump./ I'm groaning and grunting/as I force myself to crawl/while I recall recent events.

Isolation/fueled my insanity./I reacted to my mind's/incessant inclination to wander/through the fields/of soul-sucking voids. The never-ending white expansion/bleached my body—it drained the sucker/of vitality and fortitude. A faint whimper/escaped from my lips in a weak attempt/to cry for help.

Silence.

I treaded the endless,/stark-white void./Liminal hell,/eternal introspection.

There were no beings/beyond the endless horizon/to answer my call. I couldn't escape myself/as I was submerged/in the healing suffocation/ of divine isolation./My body was at the crossroads/of Miller and Sierra Avenue,/but my mind was held at ransom/by the ether, which bartered/with my tattered rationale.

I frantically searched/for a morsel of distraction,/but my line of sight/ would go hungry that night/without a glamour to fill it. In that space,/ my thoughts raced,/and my eyes were forced to face/anxiety.

There was no remedy,/rationality,/or mentality/to soothe/that anxiety. I could only wait/for it to pass over/and leave me be/until the next time/ it creeps over/my conscious horizon.

Back on the pavement,/it occurs to me,/help is not on the way./As a drizzle of rain/lands on my skin,/I position my hands/to push myself forward/ as the next memory kicks in...

"Do you think the church changed you?"

What a peculiar question/for my therapist to ask.

My life's purpose since infancy/had been preordained servitude/to the sanctuary of our Savior.

I was swaddled/in Christ's speckled wool,/and as my body grew,/the fleece would stretch/to fit my body.

Gray fur stuck out/from embarrassing seams./The elders taught me/how to white out my errors.

Intrinsic as they were,/I could not afford/to show weakness or flaws. My fingers were sticky,/white liquid dripping/all over my body,/and the tacky paste/would cement my feet/to the concrete.

I was walking to service/during Good Friday morning/and found my feet/unwilling to take/another step forward.

I screamed and I screamed and I Screamed and I Screamed and I SCREAMED AND I SCREAMED AND I SCREAMED AND I was met/by the chilling sound/of my own broken echo./I asked for help/and, as a cruel joke,/I was sent a swarm/of condors to peck/me out of my misery.

I stood in the church parking lot/with my arms outstretched,/palms facing Heaven./My eye sockets were dried out/from sun exposure.

The condors eventually took pity/and fed my scraps to their young/until I was nothing/but tendons and bitch jerky.

But/after reforming from the condor excrement,/I took shelter/among scraggly roots/while I incubated/and prepared for the next leg/of the exhausting journey.

Do I think the church changed me?

No./The church made a boy/whose only purpose/was to die,/and I made myself/from his ribs and bird shit.

My chest lifts higher/off the ground now./The rain is pouring down/harder now./My skin is a sponge/soaking up the water now./While I pull my body/further down the pavement/the final memory/possesses me now.

In the desert brush/I met a man: Adam.

He told me he could read/the stars like palms./Retrospectively,/I cringe at my fascination.

To command an audience,/conduct with your right hand,/connive with your left.

To manipulate naïveté,/castigate with your right hand,/console with your left.

Adam showed me Scorpius./He told me,/"She's your guardian angel,/aren't you grateful for her light?" He would then point to Saturn/and grab my ear to chew it out./"Saturn is punishing you for hurting me!/You only have yourself/to blame for your own misfortune!"/Berating me,/only to build me up/in the confines/of his garden.

Also, there was the matter of sex./His lectures only harshened/after I refused him my body./So I put out/to soften his tongue.

Perhaps it was better/to be warm under Adam/than it was to be alone/in the unforgiving frigidity/of the desert's night air.

However, I soon craved/heat of my own making,/and while Adam slumbered,/I would play/around the fire pit.

Kicking,/singing,/dancing/hedonistically./Sending prayers/to Heaven and/
my ancestors./But only ever/under the careful watch/of my mother
moon.

The last night I saw Adam,/I was praying around the fire/and moved
closer/to play inside the heat./My heart hungered/for flames. I
caught Adam's attention/and he began barking/about some Venusian
retrograde,/or Lunar eclipse,/or Saturnal combustion./Who knows?/
Who cares?

I was on fire with no plans of stopping.

I expanded outside the pit/and began dancing around the brush./My arms
spun with my body,/and my legs hopped around.

Adam wasn't much of a fan—/rather, more of an anguished extinguisher./
He threw his body/over the shrubs,/and singed himself in the process.

I damn near danced myself to death/the way I spun across the desert/and
found myself here,/stuck to the concrete,/on an incline no less. In
hindsight,/I could have packed/a ration of water.

Torrential downpour/pelts my body,/but I remain sponge-like/and take
every last drop.

Finally on my feet,/I reach the line/where nature meets concrete.

Blades of grass/wedged between my toes./I notice the clouds/only extend/a
few more yards ahead.

Atop a hill,/I look out/at the golden valley/waiting below.

Drenched hair falls/over my face,/and I can't tell/if the water on my chin/is
from the clouds/or tears of joy.

Wet to the bone,/passion burns/in my heart. It teems/with wonder, I
  prepare/myself for the valley.

May my body have the strength
to move me forward.
May my ancestors
guide my feet
down my path with wisdom.
I pray this prayer.

Amen.

Acknowledgments

First, I thank my parents. To my mom, the summers you spent supporting my fascination with literature by teaching me how to read and write. When I got older, you gave me your honest opinions about the works I'd written. I would not be half the writer I am today without your help. Maybe I'm biased because you're my mom, but you are a role model to educators and scholars. To my dad, you helped me form a more analytical approach to life that took me a while to appreciate, but, whether you're there or not, you walk with me into every conversation I have. I would not have the perspectives I do if it were not for you pushing the boundaries of my thinking. The car rides we spent discussing life, philosophy, and ethics have shaped me—they continue to do so. I thank Angel, my best friend. You have always supported me and my path in life. You've been here from the jump; you were one of the first people I showed my poetry to, and the first one to know about *Water Damage* (over four years ago by now). You've reminded me that we're still young, and we have time to mess up and make better decisions.

I thank every single one of the friends who have supported me through the writing of this book. Whether it was a kind word or critiquing my poetry, you all helped me through this journey. Thank you to the Inland Empire artists I am lucky enough to call friends and peers for teaching me what community means: Maravilla, Josué, Micah, Ismael, Cynthia, and so many more inspiring creatives. Thank you to my friends and mentors at CLI: James Coats, Anastasia Helena Fenald, Marlana-Patrice Pugh Hamer (rest in peace, I miss you), and Emily Anne Evans. Thank you to Brenda Vaca, Annalicia Aguilar, and my wonderful pressmates at Riot of Roses for believing in my work. I feel so honored and thrilled to say that *Water Damage* is published under your house.

Finally, I thank my alma mater for not canceling my Adobe subscription until a couple years post-grad.

About
the Artist

Consuelo is an Inland Empire poet, photographer, and artivist born and raised in Fontana, CA. Consuelo's work largely deals with Chicanisma, queer & trans identity, mental health, and growing up in contemporary America. *Water Damage* is her debut poetry collection, and she has many more projects to come. You can find her at open mics across the IE and LA, experimental art shows, your local public library using their free resources, or spiritual apparitions at two in the morning.

Find her at consuelothepoet.com

Artist Photo by: Josué Emmanuel Muñoz
Set Design by: Maravilla Guiles

About the Publisher

Riot of Roses Publishing House was founded in 2021 specifically to amplify the stories of historically silenced voices and narratives.

Xicana owned. Mujerista focused. For the people.

We publish books that heal and liberate.

Read our rebellion.

www.riotofrosespublishinghouse.com

RIOT OF ROSES
PUBLISHING HOUSE
SEJATNGA
UNCEDED TONGVA TERRITORY
SOUTH WHITTIER, CALIFORNIA

www.ingramcontent.com/pod-product-compliance
Lightning Source LLC
Chambersburg PA
CBHW020741130626
46554CB00006B/2097